WOMEN
GROUNDBREAKERS

WOMEN IN BUSINESS

Kristen Rajczak

PowerKiDS
press.

New York

Published in 2016 by The Rosen Publishing Group, Inc.
29 East 21st Street, New York, NY 10010

First Edition

Editor: Sarah Machajewski
Book Design: Reann Nye

Photo Credits: Cover (background) gui jun peng/Shutterstock.com; cover (Huffington), p. 16 Bloomberg/ Getty Images; cover (Winfrey) Dave Kotinsky/Getty Images Entertainment/Getty Images; cover (Gates) Brendan Hoffman/Getty Images News/Getty Images; p. 5 FPG/Archive Photos/Getty Images; p. 6 360b/Shutterstock.com; p. 7 KAMMERMAN/Gamma-Rapho/Getty Images; p. 9 http:// en.wikipedia.org/wiki/Est%C3%A9e_Lauder_%28businesswoman%29#mediaviewer/File:Estee_Lauder_ NYWTS.jpg; p. 10 Robin Marchant/Getty Images Entertainment/Getty Images; p. 11 Ron Galella, Ltd./ Ron Galella Collection/Getty Images; p. 13 Larry Busacca/Getty Images Entertainment/ Getty Images; p. 15 Jemal Countess/Getty Images Entertainment/Getty Images; p. 17 MANPREET ROMANA/AFP/Getty Images; p. 19 Jason Kempin/Getty Images Entertainment/Getty Images; p. 21 Ramin Talaie/Getty Images News/Getty Images; p. 22 Allison Joyce/Getty Images North America/ Getty Images; p. 23 Kevork Djansezian/Getty Images News/Getty Images; p. 25 (Tassler) CBS Photo Archive/CBS/Getty Images; p. 25 (Winfrey) Pan Media Agency/FilmMagic/Getty Images; p. 27 D Dipasupil/Getty Images Entertainment/Getty Images; p. 29 Tom Williams/CQ-Roll Call Group/ Getty Images.

Library of Congress Cataloging-in-Publication Data

Rajczak, Kristen.
  Women in business / Kristen Rajczak.
     pages cm. — (Women groundbreakers)
  Includes bibliographical references and index.
  ISBN 978-1-4994-1040-2 (pbk.)
  ISBN 978-1-4994-1073-0 (6 pack)
  ISBN 978-1-4994-1081-5 (library binding)
  1. Businesswomen—Juvenile literature. 2. Women executives—Juvenile literature. I. Title.
  HD6053.R35 2016
  338.092'52—dc23

                              2014050044

Manufactured in the United States of America

CPSIA Compliance Information: Batch #WS15PK: For Further Information contact Rosen Publishing, New York, New York at 1-800-237-9932

CONTENTS

BREAKING NEW GROUND

In 1825, Rebecca Lukens stepped into an unlikely role for women of her time. Both her father and husband had died, leaving behind Brandywine Iron Works. Lukens could have sold the business to take care of her many children. Instead, she headed the financial side of the business, which was in **debt**, until it began to turn a profit again. She steered the company through the tough economic climate of the late 1830s and set the ironworks on a profitable path that continued after her death in 1854.

Lukens showed what women could accomplish in business at a time when motherhood was their most common career. Many women have followed her example and faced challenges of upbringing, equality, and more. They succeeded not just as women in business but as people in business.

AMAZING ACHIEVEMENTS

In 1994, *Fortune* magazine called Lukens the first female chief executive officer (CEO) of an industrial company in the United States and added her to the National Business Hall of Fame.

According to the U.S. Department of Labor, only 21 percent of workers were women in 1920. Until the second half of the 20th century, it wasn't common for women to work outside the home.

HUMBLE BEGINNINGS

Gabrielle "Coco" Chanel was born poor in France on August 19, 1883. Her clothing empire began when she opened a hat shop in Paris in 1910 and a clothing shop in 1913. By the 1920s, the name "Chanel" meant "fashion."

Chanel's designs were comfortable, practical, and simple. They were **revolutionary** for a time when women still wore **corsets** and other **restrictive** clothing. They also reflected women's changing roles in society as they entered the workforce. Chanel's success didn't stop at clothes. She was the first designer to sell a perfume. Chanel No. 5 was introduced in 1921 and became a huge success.

The Chanel logo of interlocking Cs remains iconic in fashion today.

Gabrielle "Coco" Chanel

Chanel shut down her business during World War II.
Then, in 1953, the 70-year-old business icon made a
comeback, again making her brand one of the world's most
respected fashion houses.

MAKEUP MARVEL

Estée Lauder once described herself as "a woman with a mission and single-minded in the pursuit of my dream." From her experiences working at her father's hardware store to her creation of a multibillion-dollar beauty brand, Lauder showed the **perseverance** and spirit of a true **entrepreneur**.

Josephine Esther Mentzer was born in New York City around 1908. Her parents were **immigrants** who didn't have much when she was growing up. Her uncle came to live with her family when she was a child. He made skin-care products and taught his niece to do the same. By high school, she was selling his creams to her classmates!

Lauder turned her love for beauty products into a moneymaking business in 1946, when she and her husband founded Estée Lauder, Inc.

AMAZING ACHIEVEMENTS

Estée Lauder, Inc., had five employees and made $850,000 in sales in 1958.

When she first started out, Lauder gave women at hotels and salons free makeovers to convince them to buy her products.

Lauder worked hard selling her products—but she wouldn't sell them just anywhere. She recognized that selling them at high-end stores would reach shoppers with more money to spend. So, she worked to have Estée Lauder beauty creams, makeup, and perfumes sold only in the best department stores and salons in the country.

While her **tenacity** in business is often praised, Lauder was also a marketing pioneer. Early on, she and her husband used their small advertising budget to send out samples of their products. She gave away free "gifts" with the purchase of products, which many beauty companies do today. And, as the brand grew, Lauder herself was there for the opening of many Estée Lauder beauty counters. Lauder's business **strategies** worked. At retirement, she was worth about $5 billion!

AMAZING ACHIEVEMENTS

Today, Estée Lauder, Inc., owns some of the biggest beauty brands in the world, including M.A.C., Clinique, Origins, and Aveda.

After Lauder retired in 1995, she remained involved with Estée Lauder, Inc. When she died in 2004, her family was still running the company—something she very much wanted.

STEPPING INTO THE SPOTLIGHT

For many years, Melinda Gates stood in the shadow of her husband, Microsoft cofounder and **philanthropist** Bill Gates. She had been involved with her husband's work, including cofounding the Bill & Melinda Gates Foundation, since they married in 1994. But, until about 2006, Gates had another focus—her children. When their youngest was old enough to go to school, Gates stepped forward to fill a bigger role in running the foundation. With a degree in economics and a master's degree in business from Duke University, she was certainly qualified to do so.

Gates now has a big say in what to do with the billions of dollars the Gates Foundation gives out each year. Though she has only been in her role for a short time, it's clear Melinda Gates is the vision and heart of the foundation.

AMAZING ACHIEVEMENTS

In 2008, Gates told *Fortune*: "As I thought about strong women in history, I realized that they stepped out in some way." She knew she had to step out as well to be a good role model for her children.

Gates gives many speeches for the Bill & Melinda Gates Foundation on world health issues, such as the sickness malaria, as well as women's rights and education.

POPPING TO THE TOP

Indra Nooyi became the first female CEO at PepsiCo in 2006. Born in India in 1955, Nooyi's family expected her to get married when she finished her education. She had bigger plans. Nooyi moved to the United States at age 23 to earn her master's degree in business administration from Yale University.

Nooyi joined PepsiCo in 1994 and was quickly influential. She was part of reorganizing the company in 1997 when it sold off the fast-food companies it owned. Nooyi worked on PepsiCo's **acquisition** of Tropicana in 1998 and the takeover of Quaker Oats in 2001. Her vision of the company's future was clear, and increased profits showed she was on the right track. Nooyi advanced again and again, finally becoming PepsiCo's chief financial officer (CFO) and then CEO.

AMAZING ACHIEVEMENTS

Nooyi did end up getting married. She and her husband have two daughters.

In 2014, Nooyi was one of only 26 female CEOs of Fortune 500 companies. Here, Nooyi (right) stands with other powerful women in business (from left to right): former CEO of Yahoo! Carol Bartz, CEO of Mondelēz International Irene Rosenfeld, and CNBC anchor Becky Quick.

Nooyi changed PepsiCo's business strategy for the better. She encouraged the company to focus on offering more healthful products because she saw the benefit for both customers' health and PepsiCo's sales. In fact, in 2013, PepsiCo produced nine of the top 50 new food and beverage products. Nooyi has also worked to make PepsiCo better for the planet by supporting wind and solar power. And she's done all this while overseeing a company with 274,000 employees and more than $66 billion in yearly sales.

Nooyi often speaks in front of large crowds of important businesspeople about PepsiCo's operations.

Nooyi has maintained that her main concerns aren't always in the boardroom. She once told the BBC: "At the end of the day, don't forget that you're a person, don't forget that you're a mother, don't forget that you're a wife, don't forget that you're a daughter."

MAKING A LIVING

Martha Stewart started a **catering** business out of her basement in 1976 and quickly became known for her presentation and decorating talents. Within 10 years, the business was worth $1 million. Stewart met many important contacts through her catering business, leading to a book deal in 1982. In 1990, she started her magazine, *Martha Stewart Living*.

Stewart embodies the American business dream. Born in New Jersey in 1941, she wasn't born particularly wealthy or privileged. Her talents for cooking, crafting, and entertaining had come from her family. But Stewart also applied this creativity to business, constantly growing her company in new places. In 1999, her company was profitable enough to have its stocks become publicly traded. This means shares of her company were available for the public to buy. When this happened, she became the first female self-made billionaire.

AMAZING ACHIEVEMENTS

Before she started the catering business that would lead to her company, Martha Stewart Living Omnimedia, Stewart worked as a model.

Stewart has focused her business on traditional women's pursuits. Some people haven't supported this, saying such a successful woman shouldn't be pushing women back into their role as homemaker.

"LEAN IN"

When Sheryl Sandberg became the chief operating officer (COO) at Facebook in 2008, the company wasn't yet making money. Sandberg, who left Google to join Facebook, had some experience making an Internet company profitable. She had been Google's business manager during the creation of AdWords and AdSense, two products that were responsible for most of Google's earnings. Sandberg took her successful advertising strategies with her to Facebook. In 2014, the company was worth over $200 billion.

Sandberg is known for great management skills and makes a point to listen to her employees. She has **recruited** top engineers and executives from other companies to Facebook, helping the company grow. Her work has been noticed, too. In 2012, she became the first female member of Facebook's Board of Directors.

AMAZING ACHIEVEMENTS

Sheryl Sandberg was named *Forbes* magazine's most powerful female billionaire in 2014.

Sandberg once told the *Harvard Business Review* that she wants the world "to find ways to encourage more women to step up and more companies to recognize what women bring to the table."

Sandberg believes that working hard will bring anyone success, but she also wants to see more women in top positions at big companies. In 2013, Sandberg published the book *Lean In: Women, Work, and the Will to Lead*. In it, she describes the problems women face in trying to advance in their career while also being the primary caretaker of their children and home. "They take themselves out of the running for career advancement because they want to have a family," Sandberg has said.

Sandberg encourages women to "lean in" to their careers instead of sitting back in order to have both a career and a happy family life. Sandberg believes so strongly in her cause, she started LeanIn.org and frequently speaks at all-women business and technology conferences.

Sandberg herself has struggled with balancing her work and home life, but gives much credit to her family for supporting her career goals.

OPRAH

Oprah Winfrey is a very recognizable face because of her long-running talk show and her magazine, *O, the Oprah Magazine*. She runs her own TV network, the Oprah Winfrey Network (OWN), too. While she's a great success now, Winfrey was once just a TV reporter who turned her talent for relaxed interviews into a media empire.

Throughout her career, Winfrey created her own opportunities. She started a TV production company in 1986 and a film company in 1990. She cofounded Oxygen Media in 1998 and started her own satellite radio channel in 2006. Winfrey isn't just the face of these companies, though—she works actively behind the scenes, making sure her company, Harpo, Inc., is in charge of everything she puts her name on.

AMAZING ACHIEVEMENTS

Winfrey is the first black woman to become a self-made billionaire.

Winfrey isn't the only woman who's been successful in the business side of the entertainment industry. TV executive and Hispanic American Nina Tassler is another important role model. In 2011, she was recognized for helping to improve how women are portrayed, or shown, on television.

Nina Tassler

WEB EFFECT

From political **activist** to Comedy Central writer, Arianna Huffington has never found that being a woman has stopped her from voicing her views. In 2005, she cofounded a permanent space to share them—the Internet newspaper, the *Huffington Post*. Huffington's role as the editor in chief and president of the Huffington Post Media Group has earned her spots on *Forbes* magazine's top women in business lists.

Huffington was described in the *New Yorker* as having a "gift of listening to you in a way that makes a person feel simultaneously fascinating and foolish" and as being skillful at making friends. She puts that to good use when asking politicians, actors, and other notable people to write for her paper. Huffington's work earned her a spot on *Time* magazine's list of 100 most influential people in 2006 and 2011.

AMAZING ACHIEVEMENTS

Huffington has written many books, but her first was *The Female Woman*. It focuses on the roles of men and women in society.

In 2011, America Online purchased Huffington's website for $315 million.

STRIVING TO SUCCEED

From major fashion houses to major corporations, many businesses have been successful because of the women who lead them. However, the number of businesswomen reaching the top remains low. In the United States, women only own about 30 percent of all privately held companies and represent only about 15 percent of Fortune 500 company board members. Some women in business argue they aren't promoted as quickly as men and find themselves struggling to be heard.

Barriers still exist for many businesswomen, but the lives of these remarkable women prove overcoming them is possible. They show the importance of creating one's own opportunities rather than waiting for someone else to offer them. Their stories of hard work and perseverance are true inspiration for the businesswomen of tomorrow.

One of the best ways to be a leader is to be a role model for young people. Anna Chávez, the CEO of Girl Scouts of the USA, inspires girls around the world to achieve their dreams.

TIMELINE OF
WOMEN IN BUSINESS

1809 - Mary Kies becomes the first woman to receive a patent for her method of weaving straw with silk.

1910 - Coco Chanel opens her first shop in Paris.

1917 - World War I causes a labor shortage. Congress recruits women to fill jobs.

1920 - The Department of Labor creates the Women's Bureau to support women in the workforce.

1934 - Lettie Pate Whitehead becomes the first American woman to be on the board of directors for a major corporation, the Coca-Cola Company.

1940–1944 - More than 6 million women join the workforce during World War II. More than 11 million women hold jobs during the war.

1946 - Estée Lauder founds Estée Lauder, Inc., with her husband.

1963 - The Equal Pay Act passes, requiring that men and women be paid the same amount for the doing the same work.

1967 - Muriel Siebert becomes the first woman to own a seat on the New York Stock Exchange.

1976 - Martha Stewart starts a catering business in her basement.

1986 - Oprah Winfrey founds Harpo Productions. At first, it's a TV company, but will go on to have film, print, and radio divisions.

1999 - Martha Stewart becomes the first woman self-made billionaire.

2005 - Arianna Huffington founds the *Huffington Post*.

2006 - Indra Nooyi becomes the first female CEO of PepsiCo.

2008 - Sheryl Sandberg becomes COO of Facebook.

2008 - Huffington sells the *Huffington Post* to America Online for $315 million.

2013 - Sandberg publishes the book *Lean In* about women wishing to advance in the workplace.

2014 - Janet Yellen becomes the first women to be chair of the Federal Reserve Board.

GLOSSARY

acquisition: Something, such as a company, that's bought or otherwise obtained.

activist: One who acts strongly in support of or against a cause.

catering: Having to do with supplying food and service for events.

corset: A close-fitting undergarment worn by women.

debt: The state of owing money.

entrepreneur: A person who starts a business and takes on the risks involved in order to make money.

immigrant: One who comes to a new country to settle there.

perseverance: The condition or act of continuing even when something is hard.

philanthropist: Someone who gives money or goods to be used for the good of others.

recruit: To seek to bring into a job.

restrictive: Limiting, such as in the case of movement.

revolutionary: Involving or causing change.

strategy: A carefully thought-out plan.

tenacity: The state of holding fast to something valued.

INDEX

WEBSITES

Due to the changing nature of Internet links, PowerKids Press has developed an online list of websites related to the subject of this book. This site is updated regularly. Please use this link to access the list: www.powerkidslinks.com/wmng/busi